Stand Out From The Crowd

Without having people point and laugh

Dale Furtwengler

FAI Publications
St. Louis, MO

Cover illustration by Nicole Cooper
St. Louis, MO

Furtwengler, Dale.
   Stand Out From The Crowd: Without having people point and laugh/by Dale Furtwengler.

ISBN- 978-0692597224
ISBN- 0692597220

1. Counterintuitive. 2. Natural tendencies. 3. Opportunity I. Title

TABLE OF CONTENTS

Competing desires

We human beings are a strange lot. We crave recognition, yet fear the possibility that we won't "fit in." We want to be better than others in some regard, yet recall the painful teasing we endured as children for being so.

This dichotomy of desires is evidenced in all aspects of our lives. When I work with business owners to differentiate their offerings, their primary concern is "people won't know what we do." These owners understand that they must communicate the superiority of their offerings to avoid having them viewed as commodities, but they fear that being *too* different will cost them sales.

Career-minded professionals desire recognition for their superior intellect and ability to produce results. At the same time they fear being "too far out there" or being "pigeon-holed" because either perception would limit their potential.

On a personal level we prize our individuality—the essence that makes us who we are. Yet we understand that if we don't get along with others, if we're too different, odds are we'll lead a lonely existence.

Good news

These fears are ill-founded! You can be different and still be attractive. The key is to develop insights that others value.

You'll know that you've gained these insights when others say to you:

- You don't think like other people do.
- You see the world differently than others do.

- You see things other people don't see.
- Yet what you say makes perfect sense.

The path to developing this ability involves overcoming six natural tendencies we all possess by virtue of our humanity.

There is a seventh step to this process. It's designed to help you deal with the vast array of opportunities that will come your way by virtue of your newfound wisdom. Together they form the seven steps to becoming invaluable.

7 Steps to Becoming INVALUABLE

I don't know about you, but I like getting multiple benefits from the same effort. With these 7 Steps you'll:

- Overcome natural tendencies that plague all of us.
- Develop the skill of counterintuitive thinking—thinking that's contrary to what our human nature suggests.
- Become adept at creating simple, inexpensive, easy-to-implement solutions to problems.
- Gain influence by amazing others in ways they admire.
- Attract opportunities you've never envisioned.

The 7 Steps are:

1. Contributory negligence.
2. The persuasion myth.
3. Suspend judgment.
4. See similarities.
5. Contrarian mindset.
6. Eclectic education.
7. Evaluate opportunities.

Contributory negligence

Our natural tendency is to overlook *our* contribution to the problems we face. This oversight not only limits the number of potential solutions, it often exacerbates the problem. As you learn more about this natural tendency, you'll discover that this oversight is the reason why you fight the same battles over and over again.

The persuasion myth

As we enter the workforce, we're told that we need to be persuasive to get ahead. The reality is that we can't persuade anyone of anything, they have to persuade themselves. Many of the challenges and frustrations we experience result from our attempts to persuade others.

Suspend judgment

Another natural tendency is to judge things as good or bad, right or wrong. Judgments limit our ability to find solutions to problems and are the source of many of the fears, anxieties and frustrations we experience.

See similarities

Reportedly only 5% of the population sees similarities, the remaining 95% see differences. When you develop the ability to see similarities, especially in seemingly diverse situations, you demonstrate wisdom few possess.

Contrarian mindset

The social nature of human beings often leads to a herd mentality—group think. The consequences can be devastating. You'll be able to add great value to any group by developing a contrarian mindset—the ability to counter the effects of group think while earning the respect and admiration of others.

Eclectic education

Most of us devote our time and energies to things we enjoy. In doing so we limit our creativity and relinquish the childhood curiosity that served us so well in our early years. An eclectic education will help you recapture your childhood curiosity and the amazement of those around you.

Evaluate opportunities

As you overcome the six natural tendencies outlined above, you'll develop abilities that few possess. Others will seek your advice and request your involvement in their initiatives.

These invitations become the source of new opportunities which create a new problem—deciding which opportunities to pursue and which to forgo. Step 7 provides a methodology for making these decisions.

Now that you have a sense for what the 7 Steps involve, it's time to see how they can dramatically improve your life as well as the lives of those you touch.

Universal application

A CEO that I was coaching suddenly began to get regular job offers for more money. He told me stories about his wife and kids that indicated his relationship with them had grown stronger. He was also an elder in his church and gained so much influence with the elder board that they invited him to become the congregation's administrative pastor—a role he'd never envisioned, yet prized highly.

The fact that the 7 Steps enabled this CEO to enjoy greater success in all aspects of his life—business, family, spiritual—illustrates just how universally applicable these concepts are.

Besides enriching your own life, the 7 Steps will help you develop the rare ability to help others *even when you have little or no background or experience to guide you.*

A client's son was diagnosed with ADHD and dyslexia. As a result, my client and her son would spend three to four hours a night on his homework.

The son was nine years old at the time and big for his age. My client is petite. She called to tell me that her son got so frustrated and angry during his homework sessions that she was afraid that if his anger erupted she might get hurt. She said "I don't know what to do."

To give you a sense for how bizarre this call was, I'm a CPA by background. I had no training or experience in dealing with ADHD or dyslexia. My wife and I were not blessed with children so I have no experience with raising or educating kids. Despite the absence of background or experience in the areas of ADHD, dyslexia and raising kids, I was able to help my client.

My ability to see similarities in situations (Step 4) enabled me to relate to her child's frustration. All I had to do was recall the struggles I'd had, frustrations I'd experienced in attempting tasks I was ill-equipped to handle and the disappointments each failed attempt wrought. I remembered how excruciating it was to spend hours on end performing tasks that I neither enjoyed nor was adept at completing.

Then I recalled that when I experienced bouts of anger and frustration, if I took a break to calm myself and regain my composure, the solution to the problem became obvious.

Armed with these memories, I suggested that she shorten

her lessons to 15-minute intervals. At the end of each segment, she was to ask a question she was certain her son could answer correctly. Then they'd celebrate his success by allowing him 5 minutes to play his drums—something I knew he enjoyed.

A couple of weeks later she called to thank me saying that the new approach not only alleviated the anger and frustration her son was experiencing, she was seeing marked improvement in his confidence.

This favorable result cannot be traced to any innate ability that I possess, that innate ability doesn't exist. It can be traced to the skill of counterintuitive thinking—a way of thinking that is contrary to what our human nature suggests. I developed this skill using the 7 steps to becoming invaluable and you can too.

With this skill and your experiences with anger, frustration and disappointment, you could have crafted a solution to my client's problem as readily as I did.

Stand Out From The Crowd will awaken in you awareness of abilities you already possess. It's time to begin your journey. Enjoy!

— *Dale Furtwengler*

STEP 1
Contributory negligence

I was fortunate to learn this lesson early in life. I was 19 years old and had just completed my first year of college.

While home on break one of my younger brothers had an auto accident. Fortunately, no one was hurt. The other driver was ticketed, my brother was not. As with most high school kids, he had no collision insurance so his car was a total loss.

My parents contacted an attorney hoping to gain restitution for my brother's loss. Because I was the first in my family to attend college, they asked me to join them on the attorney visit. They obviously thought I knew a great deal more than I did. Frankly, at the time, I thought I knew a great deal more than I did. But that's a story for another day.

The attorney scrutinized the accident report for all of 20 seconds, then said "Your son doesn't have a case. Skid marks indicate that he was speeding and there is a clause in the law called contributory negligence that says if you contribute to a negative outcome, you are not entitled to compensation."

As soon as I heard those words I couldn't help but wonder "How many times have I contributed to the problems I face?" I take no pride in telling you that, in the intervening 48 years, I've contributed to *every* problem I've faced. I also discovered that my clients contribute to every problem they face.

As you explore the problems you're facing, you will find that you own a share of them.

Natural tendency

When we realize that we've made a mistake or contributed to a problem, our natural tendency is to put a spin on it so that we don't look quite as stupid as we are in that moment. It's an automatic response that's designed to protect the ego. In other words, our instinct is to protect our self-esteem, our self-worth.

The problem is that these attempts rarely work. Don't take my word for it, you know how easy it is to tell that a person is trying to cover a mistake. You also know how much credibility that person loses as a result.

Let's contrast that with your experience with someone who readily admits his mistakes. Do you lose confidence in him? Or is your confidence in him enhanced by his integrity? Does his willingness to admit his mistake enhance your perception of him as a confident person or diminish that impression? Are you more or less likely to trust this person in the future?

It's counterintuitive, but attempts to hide our mistakes cost us the credibility we're striving to preserve. Conversely, our willingness to admit our contribution to the problem not only preserves our credibility, it enhances others' trust in us. Indeed, people who readily admit their shortcomings are often admired for their candor, courage and confidence.

Benefits

In the previous paragraph you got a glimpse of some of the benefits gained by admitting your contribution to the problems you face. Here's how you'll appear to others:

- **Confident**—confident people aren't concerned with their egos; they're comfortable with who they are—warts and all. That's confidence most people wish they possessed.
- **Candid**—people appreciate candor more than we realize. One of the best compliments I get is when people look me directly in the eye and say "Dale, I don't always agree with you, but I always know where I stand with you."
- **Trustworthy**—you know how much you enjoy dealing with people you trust. You'll attract more opportunities than you can imagine simply because people trust you.
- **Wise**—because you're willing to admit your contribution to the problem, you see solutions others don't see. Others will be amazed at how quickly and easily you get to "the heart of the issue."
- **Influential**—as more and more people experience your wisdom, candor, confidence and trustworthiness, you'll gain influence. Use your influence to enrich the lives of others and your influence will grow exponentially.
- **A problem solver**—and you are. Because you willingly explore your contribution to the problems you face, you see solutions others don't see. Consequently, you're able to craft solutions that are simple, inexpensive and easy to implement.
- **Calm**—As your skill grows, so does your confidence in your ability to find solutions to any problem you face. This confidence manifests itself in a calm, unflappable demeanor. I'm often asked "How do you remain so calm when the situation is so dire and those around you are so frantic?" The answer is twofold. One is the confidence I just mentioned. The other is awareness that the cool head always wins...and I like to win.

• **Error "free"**—As you become more adept at identifying your contribution to the problem, you'll change your behavior to avoid the recurring problems that have historically plagued you. As a result, others perceive you as someone who doesn't make the same mistakes they do—you appear to be error free.

• **A mentor**—Others regularly seek your input on problems they face; they may not seek a formal mentoring relationship, but they regularly seek your input. It's another reason why you're so influential.

That's a lot of benefit from overcoming just one natural tendency. Now that you have a sense for what admitting your contribution to the problem will do for you, let's explore ways to overcome your tendency to want to put a spin on mistakes.

Overcoming your natural tendency
Universal approach

As we explore each of the six natural tendencies that get in the way of your success, you'll notice that they have one thing in common—they're behaviors. The key to your success is the ability to replace your "natural" behaviors with behaviors that are more productive.

Another way to think of behaviors is as habits. The key to developing new habits is repetition. The more frequently you repeat a behavior, the more quickly it becomes habit. Because habits are automatic responses you expend less time and energy getting the results you desire than with conscious effort.

Contributory negligence

By virtue of our human nature, we're in the habit of *trying* to protect our egos. I emphasize the word "trying" because, as we've already noted, it rarely works. Let's see what it takes for you to break this habit.

The solution lies in a careful analysis of the problems you face. Take just fifteen minutes each day to revisit the problems you faced and you'll quickly identify both the source of your problems and potential solutions to them. Here's a system that works well for me and my clients.

At the end of each day take a letter-sized sheet of paper and create three vertical columns. Label each of the columns with the following headings:

Column 1 - Problems I faced today.
Column 2 - My contribution to the problem.
Column 3 - The solution to the problem.

In the first column, list the problems you faced during the day. They don't have to be in any particular order. If it was a particularly bad day, just list the three to five most frustrating problems you experienced. You'll accelerate your learning and new habit creation when you limit your focus to a few items.

In column two, state your contribution to the problem. Do so without judgment. Don't use language that denigrates you for doing something that comes naturally; it's not productive. Simply state what you did, or said, that created the problem.

In column three, list your solution to the problem or, if the problem is unresolved, a proposed solution. This is an iterative process. Continue to explore potential solutions until you find one that deals effectively with the behavior that created your problem.

Once you've completed all three columns, explore column two looking for trends in your behavior or language that seem to create, or at least contribute, to the problems you face.

Compare column three's behaviors or language with those in column two. From this comparison you'll discern precisely which behaviors to change (column 2) and how to change them (column 3) so that you can avoid creating these problems in the future. In other words, you'll replace the behaviors in column two with those in column three.

Not only will you solve your problems more quickly, you'll avoid repeating them. Avoidance requires less time and energy than repair.

As you become adept at avoiding problems, and the fear, anxiety and frustration that accompany them, you'll discover that your mind is free of these negative emotions. By freeing your mind of these emotions, you expand your mental capacity. Here's how it works.

Neuroscientists tell us that we only use about 10% of our mental capacity. Let's assume that's true. When we're fearful, angry or frustrated much of our capacity is engaged in dealing with these emotions leaving us with little capacity for problem solving. You don't have to take my word for it, simply recall a time when you were experiencing these emotions. Isn't it true that when you set these emotions aside you saw things much more clearly?

When you're able to avoid creating problems for yourself, you free yourself of fear, anxiety and frustration and, in doing so, free up more of that 10% mental capacity.

Let's recap what we've just learned. The process takes less than 15 minutes a day. Here are the steps:

1. Create three columns on a letter-sized sheet of paper.
2. In column 1, list the problems faced during the day.

3. In column 2, list your contribution to the problem.
4. In column 3, list the solution to the problem.
5. Explore column 2 for behaviors that create problems.
6. Explore column 3 for replacement behaviors.
7. Replace column 2 behaviors with column 3 behaviors.

Use this system for a minimum of seven consecutive days, more if you find that you're not automatically exploring your contribution to the problem.

As you become adept at identifying your contribution to the problem, you'll find that you're able to see the problems you're creating and change your behavior in real time—during your interaction with others.

When you can do that consistently, you'll know that you've conquered contributory negligence and mastered the first step in developing the skill of counterintuitive thinking.

Mastery is a life-long pursuit. It requires us to exercise the same behaviors each and every day. Every time I sense that a problem is developing, I ask myself what it is that I'm doing or saying that's contributing to the problem. The answer to that question let's me know how I need to change my behavior, or language, to avoid a problem and generate the desired result. If I didn't employ that process each and every day, my skill would decline as well as my ability to produce the outcomes I desire.

Now that you have a process for replacing behaviors that create problems with those that avoid them, let's see how you can apply this knowledge to everyday situations.

Applying the concept
Communication

Problem - When I was in the corporate world, I'd get frustrated whenever I was asked how I was progressing on an assignment. I hated it when people "checked up on me." To me, it was an indication of a lack of trust.

My contribution - I had an attitude that basically said "When you hand me the ball, get out of the way and let me run with it. You'll be delighted with the result." This attitude shaped my behavior which left my bosses in a quandary—they had to wait for the result.

Solution - It took years for me to realize that my bosses were asking for updates because I wasn't communicating with them. Without some indication from me as to how the project was progressing, they had no idea whether I was working on it or forgotten it. In their shoes, I'd have been asking for an update.

That realization helped me craft a simple solution to the problem. I realized that if I made a preemptive strike—if I took 30 seconds to give my bosses updates every couple of days—they'd stop "checking up on me." With that simple behavioral change I eliminated their concerns and my frustration.

One of the things you'll notice in all of the examples is that the solutions are simple, inexpensive and easy to implement. That's the hallmark of a counterintuitively-crafted solution.

Aging receivables

Problem - A construction client was experiencing an increasing number of accounts receivable in the "over 75 day" category.

Their contribution - The vast majority of these delinquencies stemmed from the same situation. My client would land on the job site with a 10-person crew and equipment. The customer's field superintendent would request changes, then refuse to sign a change order.

The industry's practice was to make the changes, bill them, then work out the details later. "Working it out later" usually meant that the contractor (my client) waited 75 days to get paid and gave up half of the change order revenues.

My client contributed to the problem by assuming that the superintendent was notifying his home office of the changes he was making. He wasn't. In a few instances, we suspected this was a customer ploy to get more for their money. Regardless of the motive, the result was the same.

Solution - When a customer's superintendent refused to sign a change order, my client's foreman would call the estimator on the job and tell him what changes the superintendent requested. The estimator would immediately prepare a 2-paragraph memo stating "these are the changes that have been requested, this is what it's going to cost, we're going to proceed unless you tell us not to." Then he'd fax the memo to the customer's home office. With this simple 2-paragraph solution we eliminated the surprises the customer's home office people were getting.

Within 30 days my client didn't have a receivable over 45 days old, they freed up $350,000 of cash and stopped giving up half of their change-order revenues. Another benefit, one we didn't anticipate, came when my client suddenly began to get calls from contractors that previously wouldn't see them.

Sales
Problem - I generated a lot of interest in a leadership program I was marketing, but my close rate was abysmal.

My contribution - I touted the amazing results my clients and I had gotten with this program without recognizing differences in leadership styles. This oversight was the root cause of my poor sales history.

Solution - Once I got serious about exploring the reasons for my poor sales performance, I realized that there are three types of leaders—autocrats, paternalists and engagement managers.

Autocrats typically view employees as automatons. Their natural style is to issue instructions and expect employees to perform according to those instructions. Little, if any, input is solicited from employees.

Paternalists enjoy taking care of employees, consequently, they don't expect much of them. If an employee's performance isn't what they expect, they're likely to consider more training, mentoring or possibly shifting the workload instead of holding the employee accountable.

Engagement managers solicit their employees' involvement in identifying opportunities, streamlining processes and solving problems. These managers expect a lot from their employees and reward them accordingly.

My program was designed for engagement managers. The reason my close rate was abysmal is that I wasn't making this clear in my marketing messages.

Before I realized that there were three leadership styles, my marketing message said "If you'd like results like these, give me call." And they did call. Unfortunately, many of those calls came from autocrats and paternalists whose interest waned quickly when they realized that I'd be asking them to change their natural leadership style. My interest would have waned if I'd been in their shoes.

As soon as I realized that there are three leadership styles, I changed my marketing message to say "If you're the kind of leader who likes to engage your employees in identifying new opportunities, streamlining processes, solving problems, AND you'd like results like these, give me a call." I got fewer calls, but my close rate went through the ceiling.

The people who called were already sold. They *knew* the engagement leadership style worked, but they weren't getting the magnitude of result I was getting. By the way, price wasn't an issue with these managers; they knew the approach worked.

In addition to improving my close rate, I stopped wasting time with autocrats and paternalists who weren't going to buy from me. My marketing message filtered them out. As soon as they read my message they knew that my approach didn't fit their style and they didn't call—a simple, inexpensive, easily-implemented solution.

Leadership

Problem - A young, front-line supervisor was frustrated with her employees. She couldn't understand why her direct reports "didn't get it."

Her contribution - She didn't realize that she was blessed with a quick mind. She was able to assimilate information quickly and decide quickly which afforded her great success. What she failed to realize is that not everyone enjoys that blessing.

Solution - After I made her aware of her good fortune, she was able to be patient with employees who were more deliberate in their decision-making process. She was able to enjoy her facile mind instead of being frustrated by the fact that others weren't so blessed. Once again, the solution was simple, inexpensive and easy to implement.

Assisting others

Problem - I became frustrated when a client wasn't getting the results previous clients had gotten.

My contribution - I failed to realize that not everyone wants help. Some people enjoy being victims, others simply aren't in sufficient pain to want to change. In these situations, it doesn't matter how sage my advice is, nothing is going to change.

Solution - When talking to someone who's experiencing pain, the first thing I assess is whether they're experiencing enough pain to want to make a change. If not, we agree that it doesn't make sense to proceed.

Unless there's sufficient motivation to change, any attempt to move forward results in mutual frustration, a waste of time and energy by both parties as well as a waste of their money. I'm not into wasting other people's resources or mine.

Now that you have a sense for how versatile and effective Step 1 is, let's explore Step 2, the persuasion myth.

STEP 2
The persuasion myth

As we're growing up we're often told that to be successful we need to be persuasive—to be able to win others over to our way of thinking. Yet most of us have never been taught how.

Natural tendency

In the absence of training, our natural inclination is to use logical arguments supported by hard data to persuade others—an approach that rarely works.

You don't have to take my word for it; recall a time at work when you had a great idea. You spent countless hours trying to punch holes in your idea to assure yourself that it was viable.

Once you were convinced that you'd anticipated objections your boss might have, identified obstacles your idea might face, and developed ways to overcome those obstacles, you went to your boss and masterfully presented your idea.

What happened next? Was your boss persuaded? I'm not a betting man, but I'd make book that she said "I'll think about it." As soon as you heard these words you knew that you'd just heard the death knell for your idea.

To get a sense for *why* this happens, you need to examine *what* happens from the vantage point of the listener.

Put yourself in the role of your boss. You just heard a very good idea from a trusted, valued employee, yet you want time to evaluate the idea more fully. Why?

Because, despite the well-thought-out presentation, you're not sure your employee anticipated all the potential problems that could occur in implementing the idea. You want time to do your own evaluation. That's fair, but natural tendencies get in the way of that happening.

First, even though your employee's idea is very good, it may not fit into your current priorities. You intend to revisit the idea later, but the passage of time and demands made upon you often preclude you from following through.

Second, you have great ideas of your own. Let's be honest, when you have free time are you going to invest it in your ideas or your employee's idea? Yours, of course.

It's the reason why your employee, upon hearing "I'll think about it," knew that his idea was dead on arrival.

I've used a business example to illustrate what our natural tendencies are, but the same sequence plays out in our personal lives as spouses try to persuade one another on issues as simple as which movie to see, what their kids' curfew should be or whether to repair or replace an aging appliance.

It doesn't matter with whom you're dealing or what issues you're facing, logical arguments supported by hard data rarely win the day. You'll gain greater understanding of why this occurs as we develop an approach for overcoming your natural tendency to use logic and hard data to persuade others.

Before we get into that, let's explore the benefits you'll gain from abandoning this unproductive approach.

Benefits

The most significant benefit is getting what you want more often—something we all desire. Other benefits you'll gain are:

- **Influence**—When you help others see what you see, *without trying to persuade them,* you gain their respect and trust. In doing so, you gain a great deal of influence.
- **Opportunities**—As we discussed earlier, the more that others value your insights, the more they desire your involvement in their initiatives. These opportunities are a natural byproduct of influence you gained by not trying to persuade them.
- **Recognition**—Because you're able to get more of your ideas implemented, the results your ideas produce distinguish you as a creative, productive thinker. As our example illustrated, it's not a question of how good an idea is, but whether or not it gets implemented.
- **Less stress**—One of life's greatest stressors is the frustration we experience when we're unable to convert others to our way of thinking, especially when we know that our idea will benefit all parties. Learn to influence rather than persuade and you'll experience less stress and greater success.

With these benefits in mind, let's discover what's involved in overcoming your desire to persuade.

Overcoming your natural tendency

The key to winning others over to your way of thinking is understanding that you can't persuade anyone of anything, they have to persuade themselves. You'll be blown away when you discover how simple it is to get others to persuade themselves. The secret lies in the way you structure your communications.

As we've already discussed, your natural tendency is to use statements of fact (logical arguments supported by hard data) to persuade others. Here's a little known "fact": statements of fact have a 75% chance of being resisted.

You're probably questioning the accuracy of that statement, as you should. Let's take a look at the reactions we can expect when we make a statement of fact.

Scenario #1 - I make a statement of fact and you have the same facts. Are you going to resist? No, you and I are in complete agreement. Moving forward will not be a problem for us.

Scenario #2 - I make a statement of fact and you possess a different set of facts. How are you going to react now? Odds are you'll not only *resist* my idea, you'll try to *convince* me I'm wrong.

Scenario #3 - I make a statement of fact and you don't like the facts. It's not that the facts are wrong, you just don't like them. Consequently, you refuse to acknowledge them which is a form of resistance.

Scenario #4 - I make a statement of fact and you have little or no background on the topic. In essence, I'm asking you to trust me. As we all know, trusting others isn't something that comes naturally to us. For that reason, you're likely to resist my idea.

Of the four scenarios outlined above, you're likely to resist in three of them, that translates into a 75% likelihood of getting resistance for ideas presented using statements of fact. That's why attempts at persuasion fail so often.

The takeaway from these scenarios is that anytime you try to "tell" anyone anything, you're three times as likely to get resistance than acceptance for your idea.

To avoid resistance, ask questions instead of stating facts. Later in this chapter you'll learn an amazingly simple technique for formulating questions. Before we get into that, let's revisit your great idea to see what would have happened if you'd used questions instead of statements of fact to present your idea.

Let's assume that instead of going in with a well-developed presentation (logical arguments supported by hard data) as you did previously, you went into your boss's office and said "I've got an idea that I believe has potential, but I want to make sure I haven't overlooked anything. Do you have time to help me think through it?"

What's your boss likely to do? More often than not, your boss will stop what she's doing to listen to your idea. She does so for precisely the same reasons you do when others seek your help.

1. The request enhances your self-image.
2. Helping others makes you feel good.
3. You enjoy solving problems.

We feel good about ourselves when others seek our help. It's an affirmation of our knowledge, experience and wisdom. Being able to actually help them further affirms our worth and enables us to share in the joy they're experiencing once their problem is solved. Finally, solving problems is fun. We enjoy overcoming challenges and gain confidence in the process. It's these benefits that cause people to respond favorably to a plea for help, including your boss.

When your boss acquiesces, present your idea with one key difference. Instead of stating ways of overcoming the obstacles you anticipate, highlight the obstacles you envision and let your boss come up with ways to overcome them.

If there are ways to overcome obstacles that you envisioned that your boss hasn't mentioned, introduce them *in the form of questions*. Stating the alternatives you envision could easily be construed by your boss as an attempt at one-upmanship or that you're resisting her ideas. But if you *ask* whether another idea might work, you avoid these risks.

By using questions instead of statements you get your boss to think through the process, reach her own conclusions and validate her conclusions with her experiences. In other words, she persuades herself that your idea is a good one. Once she's done that there is no reason for her to have to "think about it."

That's the advantage that the questioning process has over your natural tendency to present statements of fact. There's no longer any need for your boss to "think about it," she's doing her thinking in real time—while you're in her office.

Assuming you've done your homework well, she'll see the same value in your idea as you do and validate her conclusion with her own experiences.

This combination of engagement and validation enables your boss to embrace your idea which dramatically increases the odds of getting your idea implemented. As you get more ideas implemented, you'll not only be recognized as a creative thinker (a great way to stand out from the crowd), you'll attract more opportunities.

Now that you have a sense for why questions are superior to presentations, it's time to overcome your natural inclination to persuade. Here are two options for you to consider:

Journaling

The first approach mimics that used in Step 1, Contributory Negligence. It involves investing 15 minutes a day creating a journal. Using letter-sized paper create three columns:

Column 1 - Ideas I proposed.
Column 2 - Resistance I got.
Column 3 - Questions I could've asked.

In column two you'll see a pattern in your communications that create resistance for your ideas. Column three provides alternative language (questions) that, when used in lieu of the resisted language, helps you avoid resistance in the future. It can even help you reopen discussions in which your ideas were previously rejected.

The more frequently you use questions, the less resistance you'll get. The less resistance you get, the more quickly you'll develop the habit of using questions in your communications. The influence you'll gain using this approach is palpable and highly profitable, for you and others.

Rewind/replay

The second approach for overcoming your natural desire to persuade is to replay a conversation immediately following its conclusion. I call it rewind/replay. It's the approach I prefer.

Think of it as having a tape recorder in your head. I rewind the tape and replay it paying particular attention to the:

- Times I got resistance or lost the person's interest.
- Language that created the resistance or lost their interest.
- Questions I could've asked instead.
- Times I generated excitement.
- Language that created the excitement (for future use).

I can replay conversations in a fraction of the time in which they occurred. In my opinion, this approach offers a number of advantages to journaling:

1. By replaying your discussion *immediately* following its conclusion, your memory is more clear.
2. You recall tonal inflections your subconscious logged that didn't register on a conscious level.
3. Similarly, your subconscious will have logged changes in body language that you may not have noticed during the meeting.
4. It's easier to recall language that created resistance and formulate questions to avoid resistance in the future.
5. You'll also find it easier to remember the language that generated excitement and capture that language while it's fresh in your mind so that you can use it again and again.
6. Because you're reviewing the discussion *immediately* after it's conclusion, you're able to more quickly open the door to further discussions.

I can't tell you how often, while replaying a meeting in my mind, I recalled a tonal inflection or change in body language which altered my thinking about the conclusion my client and I had reached. As soon as I could, I'd call them and say "I was thinking about our meeting and realized that..., which has me rethinking the conclusion we reached. I'm wondering if (note the question format)..., would be a better approach?"

The reaction I got was always the same. The client would say "You're still thinking about me?" which further endeared me to them. Then we'd discuss my observation and assess its impact on the conclusion we'd reached earlier. Sometimes that resulted in a better alternative, in others it affirmed what we'd previously decided. Either way, my client and I were better off for my having made the effort.

I use the same approach after exiting a sales call. If I made the sale, I'd capture the language (questions) I used that led to a successful sale. If I didn't make the sale, a quick review of the call often led to insights which enabled me to open the door to further discussions and, ultimately, the sale. When a meeting or discussion fails to produce a result, my review often allows me to, within minutes, call the other party with a solution or a viable option for their consideration.

This approach to overcoming the persuasion myth is one of the most powerful tools I've ever developed. As a result of this approach I'm able to generate a great deal of influence in all of my relationships—something you'll see as we discuss ways to apply these concepts.

Applying the concept

Before we get into specific applications of the questioning process, I'm going to share a simple technique for developing questions.

For me, developing questions is a two-step process. First, I allow ideas to come to me in the form they normally do—in the form of statements. Second, I pause momentarily and convert statements to questions using phrases like:

- What would happen if...?
- How would that work in this situation?
- Is it true that...?
- How could we...?

Here's an example to illustrate my point. I believe that it's a fact that companies using premium-price strategies fare better than those with low-price strategies. Yet, instead of stating that fact, I'll ask "Is it true that premium price companies are more profitable than low price companies?"

This approach not only avoids resistance, it allows me to discern whether the listener shares the same set of facts. If not, I can use this knowledge to explore his beliefs while searching for common ground for agreement.

One of the reasons that this approach works so well is that there is no judgment implicit in exploratory questions. Without judgment, there's no defensiveness.

Now that you have a set of phrases you can use to convert statements to questions, let's see how to apply these phrases in situations you face on a daily basis.

Stating facts

As we discussed earlier, statements of fact are resisted 75% of the time. To avoid this resistance, convert the statement you were going to make to a question by adding the phrase "Is it true that" to the beginning of your statement.

With this question you discover the listener's beliefs which makes it easier to find common ground for agreement.

Issuing instructions

We have a natural tendency to issue instructions. Instead of issuing instructions, ask "What would happen if...?" To see the benefit of this approach, let's assume that a direct report is using the following process:

$$A \longrightarrow B \longrightarrow C$$

You believe that productivity would improve by using:

$$A \longrightarrow C \longrightarrow B$$

Instead of telling your employee he'd be more productive using your process—a statement that's almost certain to create defensiveness and resistance—ask "What would happen if you did A $\longrightarrow$ C $\longrightarrow$ B?"

Asking instead of telling has several advantages:

- It shows respect for your employee's intelligence.
- It doesn't presume that you're smarter than he is.
- Your question allows him to persuade himself that your process is better, assuming that it is.
- Your question has the potential to trigger even better ideas than the one you have.
- Your employee is more likely to implement your idea since he was involved in developing it.

- He's going to feel good about his contribution to the increased productivity he's experiencing.
- If you're wrong, if his process is more efficient, you'll learn something without embarrassing yourself.
- It solidifies your relationship with your direct report.

Expressing opinions

You know from personal experience that your opinion is welcome *if* it supports the other person's position, resented if it doesn't. If you agree with the other party, feel free to express your agreement as a statement. There's little risk in doing so.

But if you're the least bit unsure about how your opinion will be received, you'll enjoy greater success by expressing it in question form such as "Is it true that (your opinion)?" or "Would that work when (state situation)?" or "How would that work when (state situation)?"

If you feel that you must *state* your opinion, one way to reduce resistance is to preface what you're about to say with "My experience has been..." It's virtually impossible to argue with someone's experience even when yours is different.

The key to the success of the questioning approach is that you're conveying an alternative idea without putting others in the position of having to defend their position.

Stating wants/needs

Whenever I hear one person telling another what he wants or needs, the expression I often see on the listener's face brings to mind the line from *Gone With The Wind*—"Frankly, my dear, I don't give a damn."

As magnanimous as we'd like to think we are, the reality is that we're not interested in what others want *unless* it coincides with our wishes.

Being successful in getting what you want requires you to align your listener's interests with your own. To illustrate how this works here's an exchange I had with a CEO.

CEO: "Dale, you missed your calling."
ME: "What should I have been?"
CEO: "A psychologist."
ME: "Why do you say that?"
CEO: "It doesn't matter whether you're working with me, my salespeople or receptionist, I've never seen anyone who can get people to act on his ideas as quickly as you do."

The reason I get buy-in quickly is that I go through a series of questions *before* saying a word. Here are the questions I ask myself:

1. What is it that I want to accomplish?
2. Whose help do I need?
3. What's in it for them?

Once I've answered these questions I know precisely how to make my ask. I approach the person whose help I need with:

1. What's in it for them.
2. The idea.
3. How it helps my client.

By leading with what's in it for them, I gain their interest.

I ask "Would you be interested in...(something I'm certain that does interest them)? Or would it help you if...(something that would be helpful to them)?"

Because my idea is aligned with their interests, they readily embrace my idea. Their interest is further solidified when they learn that it will benefit the company, and therefore, their future employment.

Before we move onto the next situation, disagreeing with others, let's take an excursion into what I believe is a common misconception about generous people.

When I said earlier that we're not magnanimous by nature, I'm sure some of you immediately thought of Mother Teresa, and others like her who have given so generously of their time, talent and resources. You may be thinking that what I just said about our natural inclination to put our needs ahead of those of others isn't as universal as I suggest.

Is that true? Are people like Mother Teresa placing others' needs ahead of their own? Is it possible that they are aligning and fulfilling both sets of needs—theirs as well as those they serve?

It's not my intent to denigrate, or in any way diminish, the wonderful work and amazing good deeds that Mother Teresa and others like her have performed. I'm suggesting that there is alignment between the needs of these generous people and the people they serve—that their service satisfies both sets of needs. The givers gain psychic rewards for their generosity, recipients receive physical and emotional support.

Can you imagine how excruciatingly painful such work would be without psychic rewards? I doubt that it would be sustainable were it not for those rewards. On that note I'll end this little excursion and return to our discussion of wants and needs.

The lessons to take away from this wants/needs discussion are:

1. Aligning interests *before* making a request dramatically increases the likelihood that you'll get what you want.
2. Everyone benefits from this approach—the individual whose help I need, my client and me.

Over the years, when I've outlined this approach to getting what you want, a fair number of people have said "That's really manipulative."

I agree, then ask them "Is manipulation intrinsically evil?" I have yet to meet a person who, upon pondering the question, decides that manipulation is evil. They realize that it's intent that determines whether the manipulation will benefit or harm another person.

Isn't it true that if you saw a toddler reaching for a pot on the stove, you'd do everything in your power to convince the child to never again reach for a pot on the stove? Of course you would. You'd want to protect that child from injury now *and in the future.*

Like any tool, manipulation can be used for good or evil. My experience has been that the vast majority of us choose to use it for good. You're already wary of the others.

Remember that your odds of getting what you want go up dramatically when you align your request with the interests of those whose help you need.

Disagreeing

There's an adage that says it's possible to disagree without being disagreeable. One of my jobs as a consultant and coach is to tell people what they need to hear, not what they want to hear. To that end, I must be able to disagree with them in a way that doesn't raise their defenses. Asking the right questions is the key to achieving this goal. Let's find out how we can make it work for you.

Your colleague proposes a solution to a problem the two of you are facing. It's a good idea, but it's obvious to you that there are situations in which this solution won't work.

If you make a statement to that effect, your colleague will likely become defensive because, as we discovered in Step 1, Contributory Negligence, our natural tendency is to protect the ego. Indeed, it's highly likely that your colleague will try to convince you that you're wrong. When that happens, you'll both be so busy defending your positions that you'll stop looking for common ground on which to base a solution.

To avoid these unproductive exchanges, instead of telling your colleague his idea won't work in certain situations, ask "How would that work when (state the situation in which you don't think it will work)?" Then shut up. Your colleague will need time to process the question and develop a response. It'll be difficult because your natural inclination will be to go into persuade mode. Remember if you speak *before* your colleague does, you've lost. You've taken them off the hook—they no longer feel compelled to answer your question.

Be patient, everyone assimilates information at a different rate. Also some people are more deliberate in their decision-making process than others. We saw that earlier when a young, front-line supervisor was exasperated because her direct reports "didn't get it." When I explained that she was blessed with a quick mind and that not everyone was so blessed, she was able to develop more patience in her dealings with others.

Another question you can use to disagree with someone is "What would happen if (your statement)?" The same effect can be obtained using "How would that work when...?" All three questions engage the listener in rethinking his position *without creating defensiveness or resistance.* Because the questions are exploratory in nature they don't trigger defensiveness, nor do they attempt to persuade. Instead, these questions allow the person to persuade themselves.

One way to assure that your questions have an exploratory tone is to entertain the possibility that you may be wrong. If you're unwilling to consider that possibility, even questions can come across as challenges. You can avoid creating problems for yourself by simply acknowledging the possibility that you may be overlooking something in your analysis.

Criticizing

You're familiar with the phrase "constructive criticism." It bespeaks good intentions and a genuine interest in helping your friends and colleagues enjoy greater success. Unfortunately, the reality is much different.

From personal experience, you know that whenever you're criticized, regardless of how well-intentioned the criticism, it stings. For people who suffer self-esteem or self-confidence issues, it worsens their pain and leaves them feeling flawed.

To avoid inflicting pain where none is intended, convert criticisms into questions. Our old standbys, or some variation of them, will help you avoid criticizing. They include:

- "What would happen if (your idea)?"
- "How would that work in this situation?"
- "Could we (your idea) and accomplish (result)?"
- "If we were to (your idea), what would happen?"

Instead of your friend or colleague feeling flawed or taking a hit to his self-esteem, he can feel good about the fact that he helped discover a better way to do things.

When you elevate others in this way, they gain confidence. The greater their confidence, the less time you'll have to spend supervising them.

That's as true for your children as it is for employees and vendors. As you help your child develop better alternatives to the approach she's using, you not only bolster her confidence, you enhance her ability to deal with any challenge that comes her way.

Persuading others

Recall a time when a friend tried to convince you to see a movie that didn't interest you. Or when, after being assured that you were buying a high-quality, dependable product, the salesperson persisted in his attempts to persuade you that it was in your best interest to buy an extended warranty. How did you react?

Isn't it true that the more a person tries to persuade you, the more skeptical you become? That's precisely what others feel when you try to persuade them.

Instead of trying to persuade a friend to see a movie that doesn't interest him, you could ask "Didn't you tell me that you enjoyed (movie) even though you didn't think you'd like it?"

Your question reminds him that he might have missed out on a good movie if he hadn't overcome his initial reluctance.

If the salesperson, instead of touting the advantages of an extended warranty, asked "In the off chance that something did go wrong with the product, what problems would this create for you?" This simple question triggers the painful memories each of us has in dealing with faulty products or services. Eliciting the listener's painful memories is an effective way to get him to consider buying an extended warranty.

One of the things that successful sales managers agree on is that, once you've asked a question, keep your mouth shut until you get an answer. Anything you say before you get an answer disrupts the person's train of thought and releases them from any obligation to answer.

That's true regardless of what you're pitching. There's no difference between selling a product or service and selling your child on the idea that he needs to clean his room.

To further illustrate just how much each of us resents being persuaded, it's helpful to recall a salesperson you resent. If you were asked to describe the person, it's likely that the first word out of your mouth would be "pushy." That's a word we use to describe behavior that is both unrelenting and insensitive to our wishes.

What term(s) do you use when describing salespeople with whom you enjoy working? Caring? Honest? Trustworthy? Isn't it true that these salespeople asked a lot of questions? Did the questions give you the sense that he really cared about you —that he wanted to make sure you got what you wanted? Did you get the sense that he was placing your interests ahead of his own? If so, it's little wonder that you'd describe him as caring, honest and trustworthy.

These same emotions are at play whether you're trying to get a friend to see a movie, your child to clean his room, an employee to be more productive or a prospect to buy from you.

There's a commonality to our humanity that makes human behavior predictable. It's the reason I can be certain that, as I outlined each of the situations above, you were validating my message with your own experiences. Through this validation you persuaded yourself that what I said is true.

If you embrace the concepts in *Stand Out from the Crowd*, it won't be the result of my ability to persuade you. It'll be because you've validated my messages with your experiences and, in doing so, persuaded yourself that these concepts will help you get what you desire.

Now that you have the tools to overcome Contributory Negligence and The Persuasion Myth, let's see what it takes to overcome your tendency to judge.

STEP 3
Suspend judgment

Before we get into the details of suspending judgment, I'd like to get your reaction to a situation one of my clients faced.

The client is a construction company. One of its employees was a young man in his early twenties. He was a rising star in their organization. When the company's sales grew sufficiently to require another crew, they asked him to lead that crew. As you might suspect, he jumped at the opportunity.

My client anticipated a lower level of productivity from his crew initially, but after a month, despite training and coaching, the young man's crew was only performing at 50% of what the other crews were doing.

The young man's boss met with him to explore the reasons for the crew's poor productivity. After a lengthy discussion, the young man said "I'm not comfortable performing at that pace."

Quickly, what's your reaction to this statement? What's the first thought that came into your mind?

In my programs, the responses I typically get are:

- He's in over his head.
- He needs more training.

- The training's inadequate.
- He needs more coaching.
- His youth prevents him from gaining his team's respect.
- He lacks confidence.

All of these responses are indicative of one of our natural tendencies—the tendency to judge. I'll bet yours was too.

Natural tendency

It's natural for us to judge things as good or bad, right or wrong, fortunate or tragic. Indeed, it's so natural that we often don't realize that we're doing it. Unfortunately, when we make judgments we limit the number of options available to us.

To illustrate this point, let's continue with our construction client example. If you thought that the young man was "in over his head," it's likely that your subsequent thoughts were about how to remove him from a role for which he was ill-suited.

If you thought that training was the problem, you'd:

- Overlook the fact that your other, similarly-trained crew chiefs were performing at significantly higher levels.
- Revamp training programs that have historically been successful in developing crew chiefs.
- Invest in coaching or mentoring for the young man even though previous attempts failed.
- Avoid the real issue—his discomfort in operating at that pace.
- Miss an opportunity, at a time when he's being candid, to discover the source of his discomfort.
- Waste time and money in efforts that are likely to fail.

If you thought "he needs coaching," you'll get the same result as you'd get from revamping the training. You'll invest time, energy, and money in an effort with little likelihood of a return on that investment.

Blaming his youth or thinking that he's unable to command the respect of older workers might tempt you to talk to his crew in his absence—an act that will further diminish his status with his crew.

Attempts to persuade the young man's crew to afford him greater respect also risks antagonizing seasoned workers who were productive under other leaders. After all, it's unlikely that you put raw recruits with a new crew chief. You're much more likely to have put some of your best workers with a new crew chief to increase his odds for success. You'd place raw recruits with your seasoned crew chiefs to accelerate their learning.

As an alternative to talking to his crew you might invest in coaching to help the young man behave in ways that enable him to command respect from his crew. As we discussed, this investment isn't likely to produce the desired result because it fails to deal with the young man's discomfort in operating at the pace expected of him.

If your reaction was that the young man lacked confidence, you overlooked the fact that he was a stellar performer prior to taking on this leadership role. The young man demonstrated a lot of confidence when he was a crew member. He excelled at that role. It's the reason you offered him the promotion in the first place. You need to discover the source of his discomfort.

My client's situation is a common occurrence. It illustrates how judgments influence our thinking and, consequently, limit the number of possible solutions we consider.

Judgments also trigger the desire to persuade others to our point of view. Trying to persuade others and making judgments are two of the ways in which we contribute to the problems we face. Here's an example to illustrate my point.

A young woman expressed her frustration over her inability to persuade her friends to change an aspect of their lifestyles. She felt that their behaviors were wrong. As you might suspect her friends resisted her attempts to persuade them to change.

She told me why she felt that she was right and her friends were wrong. She also said that she was experiencing stomach problems.

I suggested that the judgments she was making were likely causing her stomach trouble. She agreed, then asked "But how do I stay true to my values if I don't try to convince my friends to change?"

I explained that remaining true to her values meant living according to her values while respecting others' rights to their values *even though their values are different.* I told her that if she wanted others to respect her right to her values, she had to respect their right to their values.

The physical change was palpable. The tension in her face and neck evaporated. Her shoulders relaxed as a sigh of relief escaped her lips. A smile appeared on her face; she had gotten an answer that made sense to her.

At that moment she realized that her inability to get others to adopt her value system in no way prevented her from being true to her values. She also realized that she could retain and enjoy her friendships despite differences in values.

From this example you can see that judgments can produce significant amounts of pain. This woman's judgment about her friends' lifestyle, coupled with her inability to persuade them, created emotional anguish and physical discomfort—conditions that would only have gotten worse over time.

When we train ourselves to be less judgmental and more respectful of others' values and positions, we open the door to a greater understanding of what motivates others and where the common ground in our beliefs lie. These are the keys to more fulfilling, long-lasting relationships in all areas of our lives.

This benefit, while huge, is merely the tip of the iceberg. Let's see what other benefits you'll gain.

Benefits

Suspending judgment not only helps you create and sustain great relationships, you experience:

- **Options**—Avoiding the bias judgment creates enables you to see more solutions to the problems you face as well as more opportunities for future growth.
- **Fewer wasted resources**—The construction company could easily have spent countless hours and significant dollars on "solutions" that weren't going to work.
- **Quicker solutions**—When judgments no longer cloud your vision, you are able to see the real issue which enables you to find solutions more quickly.
- **Less stress**—The young woman in our earlier example experienced immediate physical and emotional relief when she abandoned her judgments and her desire to persuade.
- **A facile mind**—Judgments are emotional reactions. Dealing with emotions absorbs significant amounts of your mental capacity. Learn to suspend judgment and you'll dramatically increase your mental capacity.

Now that you have a sense for what you'll gain when you learn to suspend judgment, let's figure out how to do it.

Overcoming your natural tendency

When I talk about *suspending* judgment I am being precise in my language. You can't *avoid* judgments, they're emotional responses which means they're automatic responses and, thus, unavoidable.

In the example above, the behavior of her friends triggered the woman's negative emotional reactions. Her reaction was the result of incongruity between her friends' behavior and her values. There isn't anything she could have done to prevent the emotional reaction she had. She can, however, learn to *suspend* judgment—to quickly set aside her emotions.

Developing this ability enables you to see more solutions to the problems you face, avoid many of the problems you would have created for yourself and make your life immensely more enjoyable.

The key to conquering judgment is to become conscious of the judgments you're making. Most judgments are made at the subconscious level in the form of emotional reactions. Here are some of the more common judgments we make.

We judge:

- Statements we hear to be true or false, right or wrong, uplifting or denigrating, polite or rude.
- People as brilliant or slow, honest or devious, respectful or condescending, arrogant or confident, competent or incompetent, friendly or aloof, hardworking or lazy.

- Situations as being good or bad, successes or failures, opportunities or challenges, fortunate or tragic.

As you read each of the words in these judgments, you felt an emotional reaction. The intensity of the emotion may have varied depending upon your current emotional state, but you felt an emotional reaction.

Each judgment creates a state of mind that influences our behavior. If we think that something is good, we embrace it. If we believe it's bad, we avoid it.

When a person does something "wrong," she loses our trust and respect. Conversely, when she does something "right," she gains credibility with us.

People who share our values are good people, those who don't are considered "of questionable character." When viewed in this light, it's easy to see how judgments create the problems we face and prevent us from enjoying relationships that would benefit us. Now that you're aware of the obstacles judgements create, let's see what you can do to overcome them.

To help us in this regard, we're going to return to our crew chief example. Upon hearing his young crew chief say that he wasn't comfortable operating at a faster pace, the manager said "I appreciate your candor; let's explore some options.

- You can bring your crew's productivity up to standard.
- You and your crew can accept a pay cut commensurate with your production.
- You can return to your previous position and pay rate.

Which would you prefer?"

Let's review what this manager did. He:

1. Acknowledged the young man's integrity.
2. Respected his right not to feel comfortable performing at that pace.
3. Offered the crew chief three choices, any of which were acceptable to him as manager.
4. Allowed the young man to choose.
5. Later, held the young man accountable for his choice.

The young man chose to return to his old position at his old pay rate. A few months later he became angry when he learned that his new crew chief had received a raise, but he hadn't. He complained to the manager who had allowed him to return to his old position.

The manager responded by saying "You chose to return to your old job. Now you have another choice to make. You can be happy with your choice or you can choose to go somewhere where you will be happy." Then the manager shut up. He had placed the ball back into the young man's court.

This manager knew that whatever the young man decided would be in everyone's best interests. If he chose to stay, he'd have made up his mind to be happy in his role and both he and the company would enjoy continued success.

If the young man left, which he did, he'd be happier. The company would benefit as well because it would avoid having a disgruntled employee who not only wouldn't be producing to his capabilities, but would become a cancer eating away at the morale of his fellow workers—a situation that wouldn't be fair to those employees or the company.

Whether the young man chose to stay or leave, the result was going to be favorable for all involved—another benefit of learning to suspend judgment.

The keys to developing the ability to suspend judgment are summarized in the following five steps:

1. Whenever you feel an emotional reaction, whether to a person, situation or something said or done, pause and recognize it for what it is, an emotion.
2. Remind yourself that everyone has a right to choose the life they desire. And, unless you're willing to forgo that right yourself, you need to honor the choices they make.
3. Craft two or three options, any of which are acceptable to you, and offer them to the other person or group.
4. Allow the person or group to choose.
5. Hold the person or group accountable for their choices.

With these simple steps you'll quickly discover how much more enjoyable life can be when you don't get caught in the emotional eddy of judgment.

To get a sense for the vast array of benefits of suspending judgment, let's take a look at how universal it's application is.

Applying the concept
Daydreaming

The mother of an eight-year-old was telling me how bright her child is (imagine that). She supported her claim by citing examples of emotional intelligence which were well beyond her daughter's chronological age.

The mother went on to say that her child was a daydreamer and that her daydreaming was affecting her school work to the point that teachers were calling about the "problem."

Homework wasn't the only problem, the mother related an

experience in which she'd sent her daughter to her room to clean it. Two hours later, upon entering her daughter's room, the mother found her daughter sitting on her bed, staring into space, with no evidence of any cleaning having been done.

In an attempt to counter her daughter's "daydreaming," the mother began setting time limits for her daughter for cleaning her room and completing homework which triggered another problem.

Every time the mother established time limits, tears would appear in her daughter's eyes. When asked "What's wrong?" the daughter would respond "I don't like that."

Before I tell you what advice I offered, let's see what you'd suggest to this mother. In the off chance that you don't have much experience with counterintuitive thinking, here are a few questions to help guide both your analysis and the crafting of your advice:

- What judgment(s) did the mother make?
- What judgment(s) were the teachers making?
- Was that really what was going on with this child?
- Are there other explanations for the child's behavior?
- If so, what are those explanations?
- What can you glean from the child's tearful response?
- What solution(s) would you suggest to the mother?
- How would you avoid creating resistance for your idea?
- What result would you expect from your solution?
- How quickly could that result be obtained?

I know that it's tempting to skip to my solution. If you do, you'll deprive yourself of a powerful learning experience. Take a few minutes to answer each of the questions and you'll gain a wealth of knowledge for a relatively small time investment.

Here's one more thought for you to consider before I share my advice to this mother. There are multiple solutions to any problem or, as I tell my clients, many paths to any destination. Don't presume that because your solution is different than mine that it's wrong or less effective. You'd be making judgments— the very thing you're trying to overcome.

Instead, view my solution as simply another perspective on the problem; that way you'll open your mind to alternatives while retaining confidence in your ability to craft solutions to the problems you face.

Here's what I said to the mother:

I don't think your daughter is a daydreamer. To me a daydreamer is someone who fantasizes—who escapes to a world more to their liking.

I believe your daughter is a creative thinker—a person who seeks answers to questions that intrigue her. Time has no meaning for creative thinkers; getting answers to their questions is all that matters to them.

That's the reason you find your daughter sitting on her bed, staring into space two hours after you told her to clean her room. It's the reason why she's not focused on her schoolwork. She's pondering other questions— questions that have greater interest for her.

Instead of setting time limits for completing her tasks, have you considered asking her how long she thinks a task should take?

The mother emailed me the following day thanking me for the suggestion. The approach had worked and both mother and daughter were enjoying the result. Let's figure out why.

"Daydreamer" is a judgment that her mother and teachers were making. When I challenged the judgment by looking for alternative explanations, I realized that the child was perceptive beyond her years, which suggested that she was an insightful, creative thinker.

This realization triggered memories of creative thinkers I'd known over the years. I recalled that none of them held much regard for time or other people's expectations.

My experience with creative thinkers offered a reasonable explanation for why, two hours after having been instructed to clean her room, nothing had been done. It also explained why she was missing deadlines on her homework.

The girl's tears, coupled with her statement "I don't like that," exemplifies another tendency we possess by virtue of our humanity—resentment at being told what to do. By allowing her daughter to set her own timeframes, the mother avoided the natural resistance her daughter has to being told what to do. By asking her daughter to set a timeframe, the mother avoided the resistance she got when she tried to dictate those timeframes. In essence, using this approach, the mother was employing Step 2, the persuasion myth.

I trust that you noticed that I didn't *tell* the mother that she should ask her daughter how long a task should take. Instead, I *asked* her what would happen if she asked her daughter how long the task should take. By asking the mother a question, I avoided the resistance she'd have had to being told what to do. It also allowed her to decide on her own that my question offered a viable approach.

It's this combination of factors:

- Awareness of judgments being made.
- An ability to set aside emotions (judgments).
- Being open to alternative explanations.
- Awareness that none of us likes being told what to do.
- An ability to recast ideas as questions.

that will enable you to enjoy the success I do in getting others to act in their own best interests. It's not a natural ability; it's a skill I developed using the processes I'm sharing with you.

The more frequently you employ these processes, the more quickly you'll develop the skill of counterintuitive thinking—a way of thinking that's contrary to debilitating thought processes we use instinctively.

Here's another example of how suspending judgment can produce favorable results.

Values

Earlier in this chapter we discussed a young woman whose judgments and inability to convince her friends to change their lifestyles, put her relationships at risk and negatively impacted her health.

Her judgment served as blinders which prevented her from considering her friends' rights to different values than the ones she held.

Using Step 2, the persuasion myth, I asked her "Would you appreciate it if your friends were persistent in their attempts to get you to change your values? Or would you prefer that they respected your right to live according to your values?"

Before I could get her to consider her friends' rights to live according to their values, I needed to get her to experience the feelings she'd have when others tried to get her to change hers.

She needed to experience the resentment she'd feel toward her friends' judgments and their persistent attempts to get her to change in order to understand her lack of success in trying to persuade her friends to change.

My questions were designed to trigger a resurgence of the feelings she'd had when she'd been judged, challenged on her values, and hounded to change. She also needed to experience feelings of acceptance for who she is and what she values so that she could contrast the two feelings.

By reliving her experiences, she was able to feel the impact her judgments and persistent attempts to persuade were having on her friends. She could see how her behavior was putting her relationships at risk. With this awareness came openness to the idea that she could live according to her values and respect the rights of others to their values.

My questions enabled her to validate the idea with her own experiences. Validation is what enabled her to quickly embrace my idea and experience palpable relief. Her frustration, anxiety and physical distress abated within a matter of seconds.

Pricing

One of the services I provide is pricing. My promise to the companies with which I work is that they'll get premium prices *regardless of what their competitors or the economy are doing.*

The most frequent response I get is a chuckle accompanied by the statement "Our customers only care about price." It's this judgment that causes these companies to compete on price.

As a result, leaders in these companies often lose sight of what their customers value and how customers' interests are changing. Consequently, they stop innovating, cut services and continue to lower prices. Is it any wonder that customers view their offerings as commodities?

You know from personal experience that when you view a product or service as a commodity, price becomes the primary factor in your buying decision. That's precisely what happens with the customers in these companies.

The leadership's judgment that customers only care about price becomes a self-fulfilling prophecy. Their belief prevents them from innovating, improving customer service or adapting to the ever-changing customers' desires. In essence, they train their customers to become price sensitive. Ouch!

The way I overcome the judgment that customers only care about price is to show business leaders the financial results of publicly-traded companies. These results show that companies employing high-price strategies fare much better in sustainable revenue growth and profitability than companies employing low-price strategies.

These financial results illustrate customers' willingness to pay premium prices to get what they want (in some instances, to wait in line overnight to do so). It's these results that open leaders' minds to the possibility that they can get higher prices.

The real clincher comes when I show my clients that their most enjoyable customers and most profitable customers (often the same people) are the ones paying premium prices.

Again, I don't *tell* them that high-price strategies are more profitable than low-price strategies. I show them the financial results of publicly-traded companies and ask "If customers only care about price, how do you explain these results?"

Similarly, I don't *tell* the company's leaders that their most enjoyable customers are also their most profitable customers. I *ask* them who their most enjoyable customers are. Then I show them data from their own accounting records that highlights the fact that their most enjoyable customers are also the ones who are paying a premium price for the company's offerings.

At that point, they realize it isn't their price that's hindering their success. It's their ability to attract more of the customers who value what they offer.

As with Contributory Negligence and The Persuasion Myth steps, suspending judgment enables you to get results quickly. I trust that you're seeing many of the same benefits accruing to you from each of the steps. These benefits include:

- The ability to quickly set aside emotions.
- The ability to see solutions others don't see.
- A calm demeanor regardless of how dire the situation.
- An ability to "cut to the core" of any issue.
- A reputation for crafting simple, inexpensive, easy-to-implement solutions.
- The ability to get results quickly with little effort.
- The respect of others who don't possess your abilities.
- Countless opportunities for your consideration.

These amazing benefits are yours because you're willing to train your mind to think counterintuitively. Training your mind to suspend judgment was the third step in the process. In Step 4, you'll discover a way to dazzle others *without a lot of effort.*

STEP 4
See similarities

I can't recall the source, but I remember the author stating that 5% of the population see similarities, 95% see differences. Upon reading this, I recalled how frequently others tell me:

- You don't think like other people do.
- You look at the world differently than other people do.
- You see things others don't see.

It was at that moment that I realized that the source of their amazement is my ability to see similarities in seemingly diverse situations.

While I can't attest to the accuracy of the 5% number cited above, the frequency of comments from others illustrates that seeing similarities is a rare ability—one that others admire.

If you're looking for a way to *Stand Out From The Crowd,* learning to see similarities is one of the easiest ways to earn the admiration of others.

What makes Step 4 easy is that it only requires two things —an understanding of how your subconscious mind works and the habit of engaging it. That's it!

Before we get into an exploration of the subconscious mind and how to use it, let's examine a natural tendency we all have by virtue of our humanity.

Natural tendency

When experiencing a problem, regardless of the nature of the problem, do you:

- Persist in seeking a solution?
- Do you press harder when the solution eludes you?
- Have you, despite concerted effort, gone to bed at night frustrated by your inability to find a solution?

Welcome to the human race! These are natural tendencies. From personal experience, you know how draining and fruitless these tendencies can be.

You'll also recall that solutions to problems, especially the more daunting challenges you face, magically appear the next morning during your shower—*without any effort on your part.* That's your subconscious mind at work. Later in this chapter we'll discuss ways that you can tap into your subconscious mind to produce this kind of result even while you're awake.

Before we get into that, let's take a look at some of the benefits you'll gain from seeing similarities.

Benefits

An ability to see similarities in seemingly diverse situations distinguishes you as:

- **A creative thinker**—Others will admire your ability to see things they don't see and seek your input affording you an endless array of opportunities.
- **Knowledgeable**—Your ability to see the universal nature of

things, their interdependency, makes you competent even in areas in which you have little background or experience.

- **A problem solver**—Seeing things others don't see enables you to discover solutions others can't even imagine.
- **Efficient**—Your ability to make connections and discover solutions *quickly* makes you more efficient than others.
- **Effortless**—Not only will you be seen as efficient, but you appear to accomplish things with little or no effort, further enhancing others admiration of your abilities.

All that it takes to enjoy these benefits is learning how to use your subconscious mind more effectively. Let's get started.

Overcoming your natural tendency

In his book, *The Power of Your Subconscious Mind*, Dr. Joseph Murphy, tells us that the subconscious mind serves two functions. It controls bodily functions—respiration, heart rate, etc—and it processes data.

I don't suggest that you play around with its first function for obvious reasons. The data processing function, however, offers a lot of potential—problem solving being one aspect of data processing. Here's how your subconscious mind works to solve the problems you face.

When you go to bed with an unresolved problem, one that has plagued you for most of the day, you are, without realizing it, providing data to your subconscious mind. In essence, your desire for a solution instructs your subconscious to find one. It has all the information your conscious mind does so it begins the task of finding a solution.

The next morning, (in the shower or relaxed moment), your

subconscious mind provides the solution. It's almost always so simple and so obvious that you wonder why you hadn't thought of it before.

Here's the good news. Dr. Murphy tell us that we can be more conscious in our use of the subconscious mind. We don't have to wait for lingering problems and sleep to solve problems that plague us. We can submit problems to our subconscious mind and allow it to work on them while performing tasks that our conscious minds are quite capable of handling.

As I employed Dr. Murphy's wisdom, I've discovered that anytime I was struggling to complete a task I could turn it over to my subconscious mind for resolution while pursuing a task that I could easily accomplish. By utilizing both aspects of my mind—conscious and subconscious—I could accomplish more, more quickly, with a lot less anxiety and stress. Thanks, Dr. Murphy!

I also discovered that I can use my subconscious mind to help me in seeing similarities in seemingly diverse situations. Here's how it works.

Before engaging in any activity, whether business, personal development or fun, ask your subconscious mind "What am I going to learn from this activity that I can apply elsewhere?" Then enjoy yourself. Your subconscious mind will do the work for you.

I plant that question in my subconscious mind whether I'm reading a novel, watching the Discovery Channel, effecting a home repair or enjoying a vacation.

In each and every activity in which you engage, there's an opportunity to discover something that you can use in another aspect of your life. Lessons learned in business can be used at home or in managing personal relationships and vice versa.

Here are some of the things I learned using this simple, yet powerful technique.

Applying the concept
Home repairs lead to life lesson

I'm not very handy. My dad was an automotive mechanic, but that part of the gene pool didn't transfer. Previously, when I had a plumbing or other household repair, I'd think "This'll only take 20 minutes." It always took longer.

The longer the project took they more frustrated I became. The more frustrated I became, the more mistakes I made. The more mistakes I made, the longer the project took.

One day I realized that it was the expectation I was setting that was causing the frustration. Ever since this realization, I start these projects on Saturday morning knowing that I have all day if I need it. Interestingly, since adopting this approach, most projects only take 20 minutes to complete. The difference in outcomes is a byproduct of the expectations I set.

What I learned about expectations from these home repair projects, I now use in any endeavor I undertake. It increases my productivity and eliminates frustration.

It's also what enabled me to help the client whose son was ADHD and dyslexic. My frustration with home repairs enabled me to understand her son's frustration while learning, which led to my ability to develop a lesson plan that virtually eliminated his frustration and helped him gain confidence in his ability to learn.

My subconscious mind made the connection between my frustration and his *in real time.* I didn't have to think about a solution, my subconscious made the connection for me. That's how automatic this thinking becomes when you consistently apply the question "What am I going to learn that I can apply elsewhere?"

Thermodynamics and leadership

Before reading Brian Greene's *The Fabric of the Cosmos*, I wondered "What am I going to discover that I can use in other areas of my life?"

Entropy, the second law of thermodynamics, is one of the topics discussed in his book. Entropy says that physical states tend toward disorder. To illustrate this point Dr. Greene uses the example of an ice cube. An ice cube is a very structured state, but left on its own it migrates to the messy state of water.

After reading this passage, I added his ice cube example to my leadership programs to make a point that leaves audience members saying "I never looked at leadership that way." The following exchange leads audience members to the discovery of a whole new way of looking at leadership:

Q: What does it take to maintain an ice cube's structured state?
A: Cold temperature (pressure).
Q: If we don't maintain enough cold temperature, the ice cube migrates to the messy state of water, right?
A: Yes.
Q: But if too much cold temperature is applied the ice cube becomes brittle and fractures and splinters, doesn't it?
A: Yes.
Q: So the key to maintaining the structured state of an ice cube is balancing the pressure in the system?
A: Yes.

Q: How does that differ from your role as a manager? Isn't it your job to balance pressure in the system? When things are hectic, isn't it your job to extract non-essential work to prevent burnout? During slow periods, isn't it your job to introduce valuable work to prevent skills and work habits from deteriorating?

A: I never thought of it that way.

Prior to discovering the power of the subconscious mind, I doubt that I'd have made this connection. Without it, I couldn't share a valuable insight with current and future leaders.

The beauty is that it takes only a few seconds to tap into the power that exists naturally in your subconscious mind. The key is developing the habit of planting the question "What will I learn?" into your subconscious mind.

It doesn't matter whether you're beginning a home repair, getting ready to read a book, watching the Discovery Channel, taking a class or engaging in your favorite hobby, the key is to plant the thought that you're going to learn something that will help you in another area of your life.

Chaos triggers breakthrough

Picking up James Gleick's *Chaos: Making a New Science* I wondered, "What am I going to learn that'll help me in other aspects of my life?"

Even though the math presented in Gleick's book is well beyond my capabilities, the book yielded a very useful insight. Mr. Gleick stated that the math that evolved from chaos theory should have come from the disciplines of math and physics. Instead, the math evolved from the fields of meteorology and the behavioral sciences.

Immediately I thought "The same is true for business. To improve an existing product or service, evolutionary thinking is adequate and readily available in-house in most companies. If, however, a breakthrough is needed, most companies need to go outside, preferably outside their industry."

While I had instinctively known when evolutionary and breakthrough thinking were required, it was Gleick's book that made me consciously aware of how I could use this insight to my clients' advantage.

As in the earlier examples, gaining this insight was simply a matter of planting a question in my subconscious mind, then allowing it to do what it does naturally. As amazing as it may seem, that's all that's required. In fact, anything you attempt to do beyond that diminishes the result.

Productivity and problem solving

Earlier in the chapter we discussed how, when a solution is elusive, our natural tendency is to press harder. You know from personal experience how ineffective that approach is. Here's a better alternative.

When you don't find a quick solution to the problem you're facing, ask your subconscious "What am I overlooking?" Set the problem aside and work on something else.

You'll quickly discover that you're a lot more productive using this approach. Here's why:

1. Assigning the problem to your subconscious mind frees your conscious mind of the frustration and anxiety that accompanies unresolved issues.

2. Shifting your conscious mind to a different task allows it to focus its attention where it can produce results.
3. Unfettered by emotion, your subconscious *immediately* begins to work on the problem which means that both your conscious and subconscious minds are working at full capacity.

Not only is this approach more productive, it's immensely more enjoyable because you're no longer angry and frustrated.

There's more good news! Your subconscious mind doesn't distinguish between business and fun, it just processes the data you feed it. Here are some other ways I use my subconscious mind. Some are practical, some just fun.

Other uses
Wake up call

I haven't set an alarm clock in 25 years. I make a mental note of the time I have to be up, then go to sleep. That's it!

In the beginning I was concerned about whether or not it would work. That's why, for three consecutive days, I made a mental note of what time I wanted to be up *and* set my alarm. On each of those three days I awoke a few minutes before the alarm went off. These results were enough to convince me that my subconscious mind wouldn't fail me and it hasn't. In 25 years I have never overslept while using my subconscious mind as my alarm clock.

For your viewing pleasure

It works just as well when there's a program on television

that I'd like to see. Let's say that it's 6:30 in the evening and I want to watch a program at 8:00. I make a mental note of that fact, then grab a book to read.

Somewhere around 7:55 a thought will pop into my head "It must be close to 8:00." A quick check of the clock affirms that my program is about to start. Just like with my alarm, my subconscious has never failed to alert me that my program is about to start.

Reading for fun

Don't limit the use of your subconscious mind to serious endeavors. While reading Jeffrey Deaver's suspense novel, *The Broken Window*, I discovered this gem.

The main character received a court order requiring him to turn over specific documents. His colleagues were angered and astonished at how readily he acquiesced to the request. Later, in private, he responded to his colleagues' ire saying "Inclusis unis, exclusis alterius." The loose translation is that including one category automatically excludes other, related categories.

In other words, while he had agreed to turn over documents listed in the court order, there were items not requested that he could retain and use to achieve the goal he and his colleagues intended.

Imagine the possibilities this gem affords. With this insight you can find ways to meet others' needs while remaining true to your mission, your goals and your values.

Even though my intent was to read for pleasure, planting the question "What am I going to learn that I can use later?" I gained a valuable insight that could benefit both my clients and me for years to come. The uses of your subconscious mind is limited only to your imagination. I'm certain that I'll find even more uses in the future.

Convert your natural tendency to see differences into the amazing ability to see similarities by consciously tapping your subconscious mind with the simple question "What am I going to learn that I can use elsewhere?"

There are a couple of ways to help you develop this habit. First, whenever you're feeling frustrated or overwhelmed by a task or problem, remind yourself that it's time to engage your subconscious.

Second, use the technique for things that aren't essential for your success. As you see how effectively your subconscious helps you see similarities or deal with small matters, the more you'll trust important undertakings to it.

Finally, when you create you plan, task list or to do list for the day, make a note to plant the question just before tackling that project. These simple steps will not only make your life easier, it'll amaze others.

You're over half way to developing the skill of counter-intuitive thinking—of standing out from the crowd in ways others admire. Mastery will come as you apply what you learn each and every day. It's time to begin your mastery of Step 5, Contrarian mindset.

STEP 5
Contrarian mindset

On the surface a contrarian mindset may seem at odds with seeing similarities, but it's not. While these steps have different goals, they share a common process.

In both steps you shine a light on new information, then allow the other person to persuade themselves of its accuracy and applicability to the situation they're facing. The difference lies in the goals.

With seeing similarities, your goal is to provide others with new insights and perspectives into whatever challenge they're facing. The purpose of the contrarian mindset is to help others avoid group think.

Natural tendency

As human beings one of the natural tendencies we have is a reluctance to challenge the consensus of groups in which we're involved. The consequences can be devastating.

During a program an audience member cited a news story in which nine highly-skilled skiers decided to ski in a restricted area. An avalanche took all nine lives. Everyone in the group knew the dangers of skiing in restricted areas, yet apparently no one challenged the consensus thinking.

Benefits

The obvious benefit of avoiding group think is to the group itself. In the example above, if anyone in the group had been successful in employing a contrarian mindset, nine lives could have been saved.

The benefits to you are similar to those we've discussed in others steps. You'll be recognized for being:

- **Wise**—For seeing things others don't see.
- **Caring**—Because you help others avoid mistakes.
- **Pragmatic**—Not driven by emotion.
- **Influential**—For your ability to sway groups of people.

Not a bad way to be recognized, is it?

Overcoming your natural tendency

Group think typically comes in two forms—group euphoria and group despondency. Group euphoria occurs when an idea captures everyone's interest and excitement so powerfully that no one is considering the downside. The skiers who lost their lives fit this category.

Group despondency usually occurs when the group doesn't achieve the result it desires. Members of the group experience emotions that run the gamut from mild disappointment to fear, anxiety and frustration. These emotions often lead to inaction. In extreme cases, they can lead to abandonment of a good idea. Regardless of whether the group is experiencing euphoria or despondency, the consequences can be devastating.

In order to conquer group think, you must first develop a

contrarian mindset. If the group is euphoric, you need to shine a light on the risks they're overlooking. If they're despondent, you have to be the source of confidence and encouragement. Let's take a look at how the approaches differ depending upon whether your group is experiencing euphoria or despondency.

Euphoria
When the group is euphoric, you need to:

- Look for situations in which the idea won't work.
- Using the persuasion myth, ask "What would happen if...?" or "How would that work in this situation?"
- Continue questioning until the group opens their minds to the risks associated with the initiative.

During one of my presentations a woman asked "Dale, I do everything you said. I'm a contrarian. I use questions instead of statements to make my point. Yet, I'm not very popular with the group. How do I deal with that?"

It's true that contrarians aren't initially popular, especially in euphoric situations. It's because they appear to be naysayers —obstacles to what the group desires. Even though that's not your intent, that's the perception the group often has of you.

To overcome this impression add the phrase "Help me understand..." to the question you're about to ask. Adding this simple phrase does several things for you. It:

- Opens your mind to the possibility that it's you who is overlooking something—isn't seeing what others see.
- Makes your questions feel exploratory, less challenging, to others in the group.

- Softens the tone of your question as well as your body language.
- Shifts the group's mindset from defending to educating.
- Replaces pitched battles with constructive exchanges.

The key is to engage the group in reevaluating its idea in a way that lets them know that *you're trying to help them make the idea work while minimizing risks.*

Despondency

When your group feels down or defeated because it failed to produce the desired result, you want to be the one asking "What did we learn from this experience? What are we going to do going forward?"

These questions remind the group that they've experienced setbacks before and still achieved their goals. This realization renews the group's interest, generates excitement, triggers new ideas and inspires action. These questions have the power to replace disappointment and despair with confidence and desire.

As with euphoria, there is a potential downside initially to being a contrarian. Whereas contrarians in euphoric situations can be viewed as naysayers initially, in despondent situations the group often views contrarians as overly-optimistic, possibly even Polyannaish.

You can overcome this perception by offering examples of other situations in which failures later became successes. Then reiterate your belief that this group can attain the desired result. One of the reasons why this approach works so well is that we don't like to disappoint people who believe in us. When your approach demonstrates a genuine belief in the group's ability to be successful, they'll work hard to prove you right.   It's a natural tendency that works in your and their favor.

Since group think isn't an everyday occurrence, you may wonder how you're going to master this step. In the other steps you have daily occurrences to review to help you master that step. Fortunately there are other uses for contrarian thinking.

If you think about it, it's a rare day when someone doesn't solicit your input—direct reports present their ideas for your consideration, kids ask permission to do things or solicit advice (unless they're teenagers), friends share challenges they face or your boss assigns a new project to you. Each situation offers an opportunity to develop a contrarian mindset. Here's a recent occurrence to illustrate my point.

Members of my mastermind group were talking about the discomfort some of their friends and colleagues had expressed about networking and public speaking. One of my mastermind colleagues said "That doesn't make sense, no one has died from standing in front of a group."

As soon as I heard that, my contrarian mind went looking for situations in which that wasn't true. Almost instantaneously I thought "Unless you're in front of a firing squad."

The way you develop a contrarian mindset is by mentally challenging everything you hear. Ask "Are there situations in which that wouldn't hold true?" From Step 4 See Similarities, you know how quickly your subconscious mind can come up with answers to questions like that.

Having said that, it's not wise to express every contrarian thought that enters your mind. You can come across as being flippant or a know-it-all; neither will serve you well.

My mastermind group is irreverent, we regularly challenge each other's statements glibly. I held true to that tradition when

I said "Unless you're in front of a firing squad." If I'd been in a group where I didn't know the other people so well, I would not have made that statement unless I had first observed good-natured bantering within the group.

You now have a methodology for combatting group think —for developing a contrarian mindset. In the following section you'll see examples of how universally applicable a contrarian mindset is.

Applying the concept

The key to developing a contrarian mindset is to challenge everything. Brian Wesbury, the chief economist for First Trust, says he wants to be "the antidote to conventional wisdom."

That's the mindset you want to develop. In doing so, you'll discover, as Brian Wesbury has, that conventional wisdom isn't so wise.

The following examples illustrate how any experience can be an opportunity to develop a contrarian mindset.

Pricing

Many business leaders share the following beliefs:

- Lower prices result in higher sales volumes.
- The economy influences the price customers will pay.
- If their pricing isn't competitive, they'll lose sales.
- Customers only care about price.
- Lowering prices helps you gain market share.

I challenged this "conventional wisdom" and here's what I discovered:

- Lower prices don't always increase unit sales. In some instances, sales decline because customers wonder what triggered the price cut—lower quality or less service.
- The economy doesn't matter. If it did, Apple wouldn't have had customers waiting in line, overnight, for the privilege of paying premium prices for things they don't need. That's what happened during the worst economy in seven decades.
- If customers are more price conscious during difficult economies, how do you explain the fact that Walmart experienced nine consecutive quarters of declining sales in the U.S. during the worst economy in seven decades?
- If it's true that price must be competitive to avoid losing sales, then why is it that companies that regularly raise prices experience revenue growth in excess of the price increase? In other words, their unit sales are going up despite the price increase.
- If it's true that customers only care about price, how did Apple become the largest market capitalization stock *in the world* selling premium-priced products in the worst economy in seven decades.
- If lowering prices increases market share, how do you explain the huge market shares of companies like Kraft Foods, Colgate-Palmolive and Johnson & Johnson? All of these companies have premium-price strategies.

In addition to helping me develop a contrarian mindset, my challenge of conventional pricing wisdom opened the door for publication of my book, *Pricing for Profit*, and growth in the pricing work I do for clients.

Insight

People often express amazement at my ability to get to the core issue quickly. My contrarian mindset is key to this ability. It doesn't matter whether I'm dealing with a family member, friend, colleague, client, vendor or a person off the street, I look for incongruities between what they tell me and what I observe. It's in the incongruities, that the solution to the problem lies.

If a person expresses a desire to lose weight then orders a supersize meal, his actions indicate that he wants his current lifestyle more than he wants to lose weight. Armed with this insight, I can help him make a conscious decision about what he really wants and eliminate the frustration he's experiencing.

A person who claims to want more time with his family yet forgoes vacation he's earned, either enjoys work more than his family or is more afraid of losing his job than losing his family. Again, helping him explore the incongruities between his stated desire and his actions can help him make better choices.

Our pastor told the congregation that a seemingly healthy man approached him seeking financial help when the company directly across the street from the church was hiring. Is it fair to say that we find it difficult to help those who don't seem to want to help themselves? Helping this man see that could put him on the path to a better life.

These examples illustrate how incongruities between words and behaviors can lead to quick identification of the real issue. Once you've identified the issue, it's easy to develop questions (persuasion myth) to help that person.

In the example of a man stating that he wants more family time, it would be easy to ask "What's it like where you work? What are the prospects for advancement? What demands does your boss place on you?"

These non-threatening questions will lead to the real reason behind someone's behavior. Experience tells us that it's usually one of the two explanations cited above—he enjoys his work more than his family or he's afraid of losing his job. Caveat, if you believe that it's one of those two reasons, you're not being a contrarian. You've fallen into the trap the contrarian mindset is designed to avoid. Here's a very understandable reason for not spending time with family.

I recall a young man with rheumatoid arthritis who spent a lot of time traveling with his job. He hated being away from his family, but felt that it was essential to make as much money as possible to assure his wife's and children's well being when he could no longer work.

Regardless of what the issue is or the environment in which it surfaces, you'll be able to quickly discover the real issue by observing the incongruity between words and behavior.

Incongruity makes it easy to formulate questions to explain the dichotomy you're observing. The explanation then reveals potential solutions. All of this can happen within seconds once you've developed a contrarian mindset.

Practice this daily and you'll find that you're able to solve any problem you or others encounter. You'll also find that the solutions are simpler, less expensive and easier to implement than you'd expect. Your ability to solve problems quickly *and* inexpensively dramatically enhances your value. You not only *Stand Out From The Crowd*, you create countless opportunities for yourself.

Now that you're a contrarian (without being contrary), let's begin your eclectic education.

STEP 6
Eclectic education

One of the constants in education is that students wonder "Am I ever going to use this?" Unless they're able to see value in learning something, they're unlikely to put forth much effort. Unfortunately, most of us never lose that pragmatic attitude.

Natural tendency

We don't invest our time or energy into learning *unless* we see value in acquiring that knowledge or enjoy the subject. It's natural, but limiting. Here's an example to illustrate this point.

I always carry reading material with me when I'm meeting someone. It enables me to make good use of my time when the other person is running late or I arrive early because traffic was lighter than I anticipated. Most of my reading is non-business even though most of my clients are business people.

Often the people I'm meeting glance at the book and say "I wish I had time to read things like that." When I ask what they are reading, they list titles of *business* bestsellers. Their answer begs the question "How do you expect to distinguish yourself when you're reading the same things everyone else is reading?"

I'm not suggesting that you stop reading what's pertinent to your field. What I am saying is that it's not enough *if* you are serious about wanting to *Stand Out From The Crowd*.

75

Developing the ability to see what others don't see requires you to educate yourself in ways others are unwilling to do. If that doesn't sound like fun to you, let's explore the reasons why an eclectic education may not sound appealing.

First, doing things we don't enjoy sounds like work. Since the vast majority of people do *not* enjoy their work, they make a distinction between play and work. In their minds play is fun; work isn't.

The second reason we avoid things we don't enjoy is that time moves at an excruciatingly slow pace when we're doing them. If you're someone who doesn't enjoy your work, your workweek seems interminable while weekends seem to fly by. Even though the hands on the clock don't move any differently, the perception is much different.

These natural tendencies explain why many people find an eclectic education to be the most difficult of the seven steps to embrace. That's because, like students, they wonder "How am I ever going to use what I learn from an eclectic education?"

To help you answer that question, let's take a look at the benefits you'll gain from investing in your eclectic education.

Benefits

Once you see the benefits of an eclectic education, I think you'll agree that it's a worthwhile investment of your time and energy. The benefits include:

- **Quick connections and credibility**—You connect with people quickly and instantaneously gain credibility with them because you are able to speak intelligently about things that interest them.

- **Influence**—Credibility affords you great influence and enhances your value to others.
- **See similarities**—An eclectic education enhances your ability to see similarities where others see differences. It extends the power of Step 4, Seeing Similarities, to a broader array of topics.
- **Create memories**—When you use examples from other disciplines, especially those outside your chosen field, your messages become memorable. It's the reason why I reference entropy, the second law of thermodynamics, in my leadership program. Participants in this program remember both the insight the entropy example affords and me as the one who opened their eyes to it.
- **Curiosity**—Combining an eclectic education with your ability to see similarities rekindles the curiosity we had as toddlers. You're once again amazed and thrilled by the wonders the world has to offer.

Armed with an understanding of the benefits available to you, let's see what you can do to take some of the dread out of gaining your education.

Overcoming your natural tendency

Gaining an eclectic education requires you to invest time and energy in learning things that don't *initially* interest you or for which you see little value. While that seems like a daunting task, the good news is that it's easier than you imagine.

The following simple four-step process will help you ease your way into an activity you may not initially enjoy, but will quickly learn to love. Here are the four steps:

1. Choose a method of learning that you enjoy. While my examples typically reference things I've read, I attend seminars and watch Discovery and History channels. I also listen to podcasts and watch TED talks. The key is to find a learning style you enjoy.

2. In the beginning, limit your investment to 15 minutes a day. I didn't tackle James Gleick's *Chaos: The Making of a Science*, in one sitting. I read for 15 minutes, then engaged in an activity I enjoyed. It was my reward for investing time in my eclectic education. Quickly, my eclectic education became its own reward, especially when I coupled it with my seeing similarities question, "What am I going to learn that I can use in other aspects of my life?"

3. Before engaging in an eclectic learning experience ask "What am I going to learn that I can use in other aspects of my life?" Your subconscious will make connections for you. Seeing connections rekindles the curiosity you possessed as a child. The world becomes as new and as amazing as it was when you were a toddler. With this excitement comes a passion for exploring subjects that previously didn't interest you.

4. Don't become fascinated with any one subject. It's easy to fall back into the habit of learning more about what interests you to the exclusion of other topics. Set up a plan. This month tackle physics, the next, politics (Saul Alinsky's *Rule for Radicals* is excellent), psychology, negotiation, yoga or other consciousness training. Soon you'll find that you've abandoned your plan because other topics have piqued your interest. Go with it; life is more fun that way.

As your curiosity returns, your eclectic education becomes fun. It no longer feels like a chore. Instead, it's a treat you look forward to each and every day. If that weren't enough of a reward, you'll marvel at your ability to see things others don't see and enjoy the accolades you get for possessing this ability. These accolades are the precursor to invitations to participate in new opportunities. Better yet, you get to choose which of the opportunities you want to pursue.

Now that you have a process for easing yourself into an eclectic education, let's see how you can apply the knowledge you gain from that education.

Applying the concept

In earlier chapters, you saw how I used things I'd learned from the discussion of entropy in Brian Greene's *The Fabric of the Cosmos* to enhance one of my leadership programs. You also saw how I applied the insight on breakthroughs I gained from James Gleick's *Chaos: The Making of a Science.*

These insights distinguish me from other consultants and coaches, especially when I cite the sources of my knowledge. People are amazed at the connections I'm able make. They often say "I would never have thought of that, but it makes perfect sense." Imagine how good you'll feel when others say that about you.

Suspense novels provide amazing insights into psychology and human behavior. Each character has different foibles and different motives for what they do. Understanding them makes it easier to recognize these behaviors and motives in others.

Leading Quietly by Joseph Badaracco, Jr. offers valuable insights into how successful people deal effectively with ethical issues. His wisdom enables me to guide clients through ethical dilemmas they face.

Daniel Kahneman's *Thinking Fast and Slow* provides great insights into why we buy into misinformation and how to avoid that trap. It's another tool in my toolbox to help my clients.

Robert Cialdini's *Influence: Science and Practice* proves to be invaluable in helping my clients get higher prices regardless of what their competitors or the economy are doing.

These are but a few of the benefits I gained from applying my eclectic education. You'll find similar benefits from yours.

Connection and credibility

Another benefit of an eclectic education is that it enables you to connect and gain credibility with others quickly. One of my most vivid memories of this occurred during a presentation in which I recounted the entropy example.

As soon as I began this example, a gentlemen near the front of the room began smiling, his face lit up and his focus became more intense. At the end of the program, he raced up to me to share ideas about other ways in which I could use and extend that example. He also referred me to other books on the topic. The man was a biochemist.

Using this example helped me gain instant connection *and credibility* with him even though I have very limited knowledge of entropy or his field. You can achieve that same connection and credibility, all that's required is 15 minutes a day learning something that didn't initially interest you. Isn't it a small price to pay to for a life-long competitive advantage?

Versatility

Throughout the book I've cited examples highlighting the

broad array of issues I've faced and the solutions I effected as a result of having developed the skill of counterintuitive thinking. My eclectic education is essential in helping me deal with so many disparate issues. Yours will do the same for you.

Your ability to help others will become equally versatile as you become knowledgable about a broader array of topics. It's this ability to deal with such a broad array of issues that amazes others in ways they admire.

When you use this ability to promote the welfare of others, you become invaluable to them. In return, they reward you with countless opportunities—all for an investment of 15 minutes a day. There's no better investment you'll make than in yourself. It's the only investment in which you have complete control over the result.

You now have the tools you need to overcome six of the most debilitating natural tendencies we possess by virtue of our humanity. These are the greatest obstacles to the success we so richly deserve.

None of the first six steps requires more than 15 minutes a day for you to overcome these tendencies. Within seven weeks you'll have made great strides in mastering the skill of counter-intuitive thinking. Like any skill, it needs to be utilized every day otherwise the skill wanes. I employ all six steps everyday. Why? In part, because it makes me feel good about myself; it also pays handsomely in terms of opportunity.

You'll be amazed at the number of opportunities offered to you as a result of having developed the skill of counterintuitive thinking. That's good news, but it also creates a new problem for you—how do you choose which opportunities to pursue and which to forgo? Step 7, Evaluate opportunities, simplifies the decision-making process for you. Let's see what's involved.

STEP 7
Evaluate opportunities

Earlier in this book, I cited a CEO I coached who regularly got job offers for more money. You'll recall that he'd gained so much influence with the elder board of his church that they'd invited him to be their administrative pastor? His experience illustrates the type of dilemma you'll face when opportunities present themselves.

He enjoyed business and was successful at it. He was also deeply religious which made the administrative pastor role very attractive to him. His dilemma was that he knew he couldn't perform both roles simultaneously; he had to choose one or the other. Before we get into his decision or how he arrived at it, let's explore our natural tendency in situations like this.

Natural tendency

When presented with several intriguing choices, our natural tendency is inaction. We don't do this intentionally, instead we get trapped into a continuous loop of evaluating the advantages and disadvantages of each opportunity. Each has its appeal as well as less attractive elements to it. In this state we experience fear, anxiety and frustration.

We're afraid of making the wrong choice, anxious about the consequences if we do and frustrated because we don't have a methodology for simplifying the decision.

That's a heavy burden for anyone to carry. Fortunately, it doesn't have to be that way. The solution is much simpler than you might imagine.

Before we get into the solution, let's see what benefits you gain from having a methodology for evaluating opportunities.

Benefits

With the solution, you'll gain:

- **Freedom**—Freedom from the debilitating emotions of fear, anxiety and frustration.
- **Joy**—Joy over having a methodology for making quick, yet well-thought-out decisions for your future.
- **Confidence**—Conscious decisions enhance confidence while emotionally-driven choices create doubt, fear and anxiety.
- **Quick results**—Being able to decide quickly enables you to enjoy the benefits of your choice more quickly.
- **Fewer regrets**—A conscious decision about what you want increases the likelihood of your success in that decision. Consequently, you experience fewer regrets.
- **Even more opportunities**—With increased confidence and greater success, you'll be presented with even more opportunities.

Now that you have a sense for what a system for evaluating opportunities will do for you, let's see what that system entails.

Overcoming your natural tendency

Absent a methodology for evaluating opportunities, you'll find yourself in a continuous loop, an eddy if you will, in which you continuously cycle between seeing the advantages and the disadvantages of each opportunity.

Here's the approach I recommended to the CEO who was enjoying success in so many aspects of his life. As you can see the approach involves a series of questions that were designed to help him, and you, make conscious decisions more quickly.

1. What do I want out of life? Is it fame, fortune, a loving family and comfortable lifestyle or something else?
2. Does this opportunity help me achieve that life? If not, why am I considering it?
3. What impact will choosing this opportunity have on my family? Will it provide what they want out of life? It's very difficult to be successful without the support of your family. That's why it's essential to consider their needs as well as your own.
4. How many lives can I favorably impact if I choose this opportunity? Your value is determined by how many people you help.
5. What's the likelihood this opportunity will be available to me in the future? It's easier to postpone than forgo an opportunity. If you know that an opportunity will be available to you in the future, choose one with a shorter shelf life.

As you can see, these questions are designed to enable you to be more conscious in your decision making. Most of us make our decisions based on the emotions we experience.

It's the reason why we often regret the decisions we make. Our emotions are good at helping us survive imminent dangers, but lousy at helping us make informed decisions.

Now that you have a methodology for overcoming your natural tendency toward inaction, let's see how our CEO used this system in making his decision.

Applying the concept

Here's how the CEO responded to each of these questions:

1. He wanted to make a difference in other people's lives.
2. He found both roles, CEO and Administrative Pastor, to be equally appealing. He believed that he could make a difference in others' lives in either role.
3. The financial rewards were better as CEO which would afford his family a more comfortable lifestyle. When he asked his wife, who was also deeply religious, what she wanted she said she'd be content with either choice. She reminded him that they were very happy before the income his CEO role afforded.
4. Since the congregation was relatively small, he decided that he could have a greater impact in business.
5. He believed that the administrative pastor role would be available to him in the future.

Based on this analysis he decided to remain in his role as CEO. The answers to questions four and five tipped the scales. Once he realized that he could help more people in his business role and that the administrative pastor position was likely to be available in the future, it was an easy choice.

His analysis of these two opportunities, using the questions outlined above, enabled him to make a conscious decision that was consistent with his mission in life. Consequently, he was no longer plagued with the doubts that normally accompany emotionally-driven choices. Instead, he was comfortable and confident in his decision to continue in his role as CEO and, as a result, experienced joy instead of doubt, purpose instead of fear, anxiety and frustration. Imagine how much more fun and exciting your life will be when you're no longer plagued by the doubts and concerns that opportunities previously triggered.

Now that you have the tools to create and evaluate new opportunities for yourself, I'd like to share my wish for you and your children.

My wish for you

I want you to have a life in which you no longer pursue opportunities, they pursue you.

I want your world to become a playground filled with toys you never envisioned and you get to choose which toys you want to play with and which to ignore. When you find that a toy no longer intrigues you, you'll quickly set it aside knowing that there are always more toys awaiting you.

That's my wish for you.

For your children

Imagine what a leg up your children would have in life if they learned to think counterintuitively. It's more likely and much easier to achieve than you might think.

Natural tendency

As adults we tend to underestimate the learning capacity of children. We're also unaware of how much attention they pay to what we do and say. These natural tendencies prevent our children from enjoying the potential that exists within them. To illustrate how great a child's capacity for learning really is, I'll share a call I got from my CEO client.

He was laughing as he called. He said "Dale, you're going to love this. My 10-year-old son and I were riding in my truck when he asked 'Dad, did you ever do anything really stupid?' "

The CEO, choking back a desire to laugh, responded "Yes, son, I have. What did you do?" His son told him.

He asked his son "What should you have done?" The son answered appropriately. Then the CEO asked his son "How are you going to fix it?" His son suggested a well-thought-out solution. He congratulated his son on having recognized his mistake and having come up with a solution to the problem he had created.

88

What prompted the CEO's call to me was his amazement over the fact that his *10-year-old son* was using Step 4, the Persuasion Myth, to affirm his thinking and, hopefully, mitigate his punishment. The son was successful in achieving both.

His father didn't see any reason to punish him for making a mistake when he'd readily admitted the mistake (contributory negligence), had developed a well-reasoned solution and was willing to take action to rectify his mistake.

The CEO and I both were intrigued by the fact that his son had developed the skill of counterintuitive thinking by simply observing his dad's behavior. The CEO confirmed that he had never "taught" any of the seven steps to his son, yet his son had utilized two of them in this dialogue with his dad. The son gleaned them from his father's interactions with others.

Imagine how much more successful this young man will be for having learned these lessons so early in life. Not only will he be more successful, he'll enjoy his life much more. The key to helping your children enjoy that life is to model the behavior. Children learn more by observing our behavior than listening to our words. They're savvy enough to know that actions speak louder than words which is why they trust our behaviors more than what we say.

Benefits

The benefits your children will gain are the same benefits you experience. They're outlined in each of the sections above. In addition, you gain the joy and satisfaction that your family will enjoy these benefits for generations to come. Now that's a legacy worth leaving.

Overcoming your natural tendency

It's natural to underestimate your child's ability. You don't do it intentionally. You simply recall how long it took you to learn some of life's lessons and assume that the learning curve is steep for everyone. You're overlooking the fact that the role models in your life didn't have the good fortune to have learned these lessons. If they had, and had modeled the behavior, you would have seen how effective they were, adopted them and enjoyed a richer fuller life than you already have.

The most effective way to teach your kids is always by example. When they see you enjoying a life rich in friendships and opportunities, as they observe others' admiration of your capabilities, they'll readily emulate what they're seeing just as the CEO's son did.

Remember, people tend to resist what we tell them whereas they readily accept what they observe. The resistance begins at age 2 when we begin to assert our independence and becomes more pronounced as we gain knowledge and experience. Don't *tell* your kids what the seven steps are, live them. When they ask about why you do what you do or why you gain so much from what you do, tell them. They've given you permission to do so.

Explain, but don't press. One sure way to kill their interest is to press them to behave according to the seven steps. When you explain the step they inquired about, don't press them to employ it. They'll resist. Instead allow them time to validate what you've said with their own experiences. Once they do that, they'll embrace what you've told them and use it to their advantage.

Yes, I know this requires patience at a time when what you want most is for your child to enjoy the benefits NOW. The reality is that they'll enjoy the benefits more quickly when you don't press. Again, it's counterintuitive, but overcoming your desire to impose your wisdom on your children will accelerate their adoption of that wisdom.

Applying the concept

Our children absorb more than we realize when they're in our presence. Here's a personal example to illustrate my point.

Three of my buddies and I rented an apartment instead of living in the dorm. We had discussed who was going to be the cook, but no one volunteered for the role.

The first morning we each fixed our own breakfast. Upon seeing the results, I was elected cook—a decision I still find amazing some 40+ years later. It wasn't gourmet cooking, but I didn't send anyone to the hospital.

During my first visit with my parents after moving into the apartment, my mom asked who was doing the cooking. I told her I was. She laughed as she asked "Really, who's doing the cooking? When I assured her that I was, she asked "What did you fix?" When I told her she asked, "How did you fix it?"

Upon hearing my menu and approach to preparing it she said, "I had no idea that you were paying that much attention while I was cooking." She had never shown me how to cook any of the meals I'd prepared. I knew what to do because I paid attention to what she was doing while preparing the dishes I enjoyed most.

The point is that you don't have to do anything special to teach your kids valuable lessons. All you have to do is behave consistently in ways that provide valuable lessons to them. The best way to teach kids the seven steps is to live them.

Here's another example to illustrate how behavior trumps telling. I worked at a Piggly Wiggly store while attending high school. We always received a huge delivery early on Saturday morning in anticipation of the weekend rush. When we were finished unloading the truck, we got a 15-minute break.

Occasionally we extended the break to 20 or 25 minutes. The manager never complained about, or chastised us for, the longer breaks because he knew that once we began stocking shelves we'd accomplish the task quickly.

From that manager's behavior I learned a valuable lesson— don't manage time, manage productivity. As long as there was product on the shelf for customers to buy, he didn't care how long our breaks were. He never expressed that verbally, but the message was loud and clear through his behavior.

Children learn from their dealings with us. Remember the young mother who thought her child was a daydreamer. Her daughter experienced being told what to do and didn't like it. She also got to experience what it was like to control her own schedule—a much more enjoyable experience. Which of these behaviors do you think the daughter is likely to emulate in her dealings with others?

Modeling behavior works equally well in teaching each of the seven steps. When your interests are eclectic, when you are genuinely excited by and curious about different topics, your children are more likely to retain their childhood curiosity.

When you willingly admit your contribution to problems, your children will as well. When, in lieu of judging, you respect everyone's right to their values and beliefs, your child will too. Become more adept at seeing similarities in diverse situations, they'll look for those as well. Display a contrarian mindset and your children learn to challenge what they hear, read or see.

With these seven steps, with the skill of counterintuitive thinking, you have the power to brighten your children's future as well as your own. My brothers and I had the good fortune to learn valuable lessons from our parents—not through formal training, but by observing how they lived. From their behavior we learned to be confident, self-sufficient, independent, caring members of society.

As a result, we've each enjoyed success in whatever we've chosen to do and we are blessed to be part of one of the most loving families I've ever encountered. That's my wish for you, your children and countless generations to come. I want these seven steps to bring you love, joy and countless opportunities.

About the author

Dale Furtwengler helps his clients enjoy greater personal, professional, and business success.

A former CFO, Dale has been a guest speaker at Webster and Lindenwood Universities and Fontbonne College. He also co-hosted Lindenwood University's Business Roundtable TV program. Bisk Education Services interviewed Dale on several occasions for their continuing education series for CPAs and he's been quoted in the *Harvard Management Communication Letter*. He was also a Missouri Quality Award Examiner.

In addition to *Stand Out From the Crowd* Dale is the author of *Lead a Life of Confidence, Become a Maverick, Pricing for Profit, The 10-Minute Guide to Performance Appraisals, The Uniqueness Myth*, and *Making the Exceptional Normal*.

Dale is an adjunct faculty member at the University of Missouri–St. Louis and lives in St. Louis, MO.

For information on how you can live more joyfully, visit: http://TheLifeOthersDesire.com.

www.ingramcontent.com/pod-product-compliance
Lightning Source LLC
Chambersburg PA
CBHW071015040426
42443CB00007B/785